IT'S NOT ABOUT RATE

THE RIGHT WAY TO GET A MORTGAGE

RICHARD COHEN

Bloomington, IN

authorHOUSE®

Milton Keynes, UK

AuthorHouse™
1663 Liberty Drive, Suite 200
Bloomington, IN 47403
www.authorhouse.com
Phone: 1-800-839-8640

AuthorHouse™ UK Ltd.
500 Avebury Boulevard
Central Milton Keynes, MK9 2BE
www.authorhouse.co.uk
Phone: 08001974150

First published by AuthorHouse 3/5/2007

ISBN: 978-1-4259-9178-4 (sc)

Printed in the United States of America
Bloomington, Indiana

This book is printed on acid-free paper.

For Amy,
always helping me jump

and for Lilly,
the reason I jump

ACKNOWLEDGEMENTS

First, I want to thank Steve Calk for giving me the opportunity in this field. Because of his constant trust and confidence in my ability to be successful in this industry I am now able to write this book. Steve has always pushed me to find ways to be a better loan officer and a better person at the same time.

I also want to thank Laura Watson, Bernie Miller, Suellen Long, Bill Conaghan, and Linda Feinstein for their help with the manuscript.

Mary Jane Grinstead has been a blessing to me in providing guidance for the writing of the book.

I want to thank Katherine Stoica for her patience and honesty.

I want to express my deepest thanks to Barry Moltz who, as everyone who knows him knows very well, is one of the most giving people I have met. Barry will tell me the truth and will always make himself available to work through an idea or problem. To Barry: I will reach my dream.

I need to thank all of my colleagues and friends in the industry. You are the ones who push me and teach me the right way to do my job.

Last, the most heartfelt thanks to every homebuyer with whom I have had a conversation about mortgage-related matters. With each conversation I have been asked at least one question that has forced me to think and feel from a perspective that I had never imagined. This is the side of the industry, I believe, that many loan officers disregard, and for which I feel most thankful.

CONTENTS

Introduction:
Bungee Jumping

In The Beginning There Was
Fear: Who, Me, Nervous?

Amy and I are on our honeymoon in Queenstown, New Zealand, the extreme adventure capital of the world. We planned to tour the vineyards on this one particular day, but before we arrive at the first of these we pass the lowest bungee-jumping bridge in the city. We stop to watch a few people jump off the bridge, which is suspended over a small, quiet river, and I think, "Not bad at all. I could do this."

Later, we go to the registration office to sign up. A half-dozen television monitors running videos of dozens of activities accentuate the excitement in the store. Amy and I stroll around and stop in front of the video of Nevis, the big mamma of the bungee jumps—134 meters (fifty stories!) of jumping and falling through air.

Hoping to wish away the inevitable, I close my eyes as Amy says, "We have to do it. It would kill me if we didn't try," and I respond in my head, "Yeah, and it's going to kill me for sure if we do."

Thus began our first argument as a married couple.

After a full day of ridicule and harassment, I agree to do the jump. Amy's words of wisdom echo in my head. "Everything is going to be fine. They know what they're doing. You have to trust the equipment."

We sign away any legal rights to our present lives. Then, with about twenty other thrill-seekers, we ride in a minivan up a narrow road that twists and turns around a cliff (though it seemed more like a mountain at the time).

At the top we are weighed, as the order of jumping is heaviest to lightest weight. I am lucky number three. We take a cable car across a ravine to another, *larger* cable car suspended above the ravine from which we will jump.

Amy and I look at each other and then down at the ravine, trying to locate the semblance of some actual moving water, and then back at each other. You guessed it. I am starting to get a little more than nervous, and there is no confusion about what I mean by that word.

The first jumper is suited up, strapped to the bungee, and carefully escorted to the ledge that frighteningly resembles a gangplank. He is seconds away from jumping fifty stories straight down.

"What if the cord breaks?" I think I'm talking to myself, but apparently I actually speak out loud because the bungee instructor quietly whispers, "It's not a cord. It's a bungee. And we haven't had one break yet."

Having shared this useful information, he proceeds to count down, *"Five, four, three, two, one,"* and my wife and I watch number one jump and then fall like a bullet, until finally, after seven seconds that seemed to last an hour, the bungee catches and bounces him back up.

As the next jumper moves to the plank, I sit in the chair and am harnessed to the bungee. My heart is starting to really pound. They finish up as I hear the countdown, *"Five, four, three, two, one."* I watch the second jumper disappear from the cable car. Now it's my turn.

Although I can feel the adrenaline, emanating no doubt from fear, I also feel excitement. I have never done anything like this before. When the two previous jumpers were pulled up, they were yelling with excitement. I definitely feel as though this could be my last day, yet at the same time I know that everything is going to be just fine. I hope.

The bungee operators move me to the edge. I look at my wife holding the video camera and try to smile, but I can barely move my lips. My mouth is a bag of cotton balls. I breathe deeply as they begin to count down. We have a delay while they untangle the bungee.

I look down into the ravine, and the count begins again. "*Five, four, three, two, one.*"

I jump, and after a moment of absolute terror, a rush of bliss fills my body. I've never felt anything like it.

TRUSTING THE EXPERTS AND THE EQUIPMENT

In addition to being a bungee jumper, I am a loan officer in the mortgage industry, and it now has occurred to me that people describe these same emotions when they talk about buying a new home. Although I cannot talk with expertise about being a seasoned bungee jumper, I am confident and knowledgeable when it comes to the process of obtaining a mortgage, and I have to say that preparing—committing—to buy a home and obtain a mortgage loan can feel a little like the decision to make a bungee jump.

The goal of this book is to help you understand the home mortgage approval process and the role and responsibilities of a professional and committed loan officer. Once you begin to understand the terms, processes, requirements, and relationships that I explain in these pages, you will also recognize not only how the right loan officer (like the right instructor on my bungee jump) can make the mortgage process uncomplicated, but also why choosing the right mortgage professional matters every bit as much as interest rates and closing costs.

When I told friends the title of this book, some raised an eyebrow. Some raised two eyebrows. Maybe you had the same reaction.

Let me say right now, the interest rate you pay on your mortgage is important. However, many home buyers limit their focus to this one point—getting the lowest rate—when they would be well served to consider additional factors.

People probably focus on rate because it is the easiest thing to understand, to gauge, or to measure. The other variables that go into getting a mortgage can seem confusing and complicated. That's why I wrote this book.

In the next chapters, I explain why limiting your focus to just the interest rate can result in a more costly loan and a more anxiety-filled loan process. I will also help you understand the loan process from the inside out so that when you decide it's time to buy a house, you will proceed as an educated and confident borrower.

Because so much of this process is behind the scenes, once a homebuyer makes an offer and writes a contract to purchase a house—the largest and most significant investment that most people ever make—he or she has to trust that the loan process will go smoothly and be trouble-free.

Despite the churn of excitement and fear, the borrower has to believe that the loan will be approved and that the money will actually show up when it's time to pay the seller for the house. In this way it is like me taking that bungee jump. You have to work through the anxiety and nervousness to get to the joy and excitement.

You have to find an expert to guide you through, and then you have to trust the equipment.

Chapter 1:
Preparation is the Key

Here's the Good News

There are programs for just about anyone who wants to get a mortgage. Lower than excellent credit score? No problem. Can't verify income? No problem. Can't verify assets? No problem. No employment verification? No problem. Can't verify income, assets, and employment? Difficult, but still very possible. Want to buy a home in Switzerland? Can't do that. You'll need cash.

This book teaches you what you need to know about the mortgage process from an insider's point of view. Your first lesson is to accept the fact that no matter what the advertisements say, the process is not so simple, especially if your financial situation is less than perfect. There are programs to accommodate less-than-perfect financial situations, but the programs have more complicated guidelines. You will need an expert to guide you through the steps.

Your second lesson: seemingly small mistakes can cost the borrower big money. For example, a buyer may find the lowest rate, but if the loan does not close on time, or at all, unplanned expenses could be significant.

Your third lesson is that as a borrower, you do not have to understand everything there is to know about getting a mortgage—as long as you have chosen your loan officer wisely. It is the loan officer's job to take the details of your situation, understand your personal goals, and match them to the best loan product for you.

A loan officer is a person who works for a lending institution and meets with people to help them obtain a loan. They have a knowledge and familiarity with various loan programs. In many states, loan officers must be licensed. Your loan officer will guide you through every step of the application, underwriting, and approval process so that your loan will be in place exactly when you need it to close on your new home.

MORTGAGE PRE-APPROVAL

Many borrowers assume that they can find a house, write a contract for a property, and then select a loan officer and get approved for a mortgage in the time frame specified in their purchase contract. Sometimes this works, but signing a purchase agreement before knowing that you qualify for a loan is like filling the roller with paint before you've plastered and sanded the walls.

Now is the time, before fantasizing about a dream home and before looking at any properties, to determine the highest amount of money that you want to spend per month. How much do you really want to spend every thirty days on your total mortgage obligation? Remember that unlike a landlord who may let you pay your rent a few days late, mortgage lenders may charge hefty fees for payments that are even one day overdue.

You may be making this decision on your own, but if a co-borrower is going to share the responsibility of the mortgage payment, you should discuss this question and jointly decide on a number together.

I encourage my clients to write down a complete budget of all expenses, leaving the anticipated mortgage payment until last. Once you do this, you are much more prepared to think about owning a home. This is the first and most important element of the home-buying process.

What Is This Thing Called a Mortgage?

The origins of the word come from the old French *mort* (dead) and *gage* (pledge), which simply meant that if a person borrowing money did not pay the debt, then the deal was dead, or, more happily, once the debt was repaid, then the debt itself was dead (fulfilled).

Today, if you want to buy a home either you have the cash to pay for it outright or you must obtain a loan. A mortgage (an actual paper document) is your legal and binding pledge to honor the terms of the loan and to repay the money that you borrow plus interest. The property that you are purchasing serves as collateral, which means that if for some reason you don't pay your loan, the lender has the right to seize your property.

The lender sets up a payment schedule, which usually calls for a monthly payment, and typically sends you a book of twelve payment coupons, one for each month of the year. A coupon from your payment book will have information that looks something like this:

Principal	$ 211
Interest	$ 899
Tax	$ 125
Insurance	$ 98
Total	$ 1,333

3

This full payment of principal, interest, taxes, and insurance is know as PITI and is important information when your lender qualifies you for a loan.

The *principal* is the portion of the total money loaned that you pay back every month. The *interest* is the money that the lender charges to make the loan. The higher the interest rate, the more money you pay to the bank and the less (of your payment) that goes to principal. Most home loans are amortized (established in installment plans) over thirty years. In earlier years of the loan, most of the monthly payment goes to pay interest, because lenders make their money up front. As the years pass, a greater portion of the monthly payment goes toward the principal, and in the last few years of the loan, borrowers will be paying mostly principal.

You will also pay *taxes* to an escrow account kept by the lender. The lender holds the monthly payment in this escrow account so that when the tax bill comes due, the full amount is available, and the lender can pay the taxes for you.

If you are purchasing a single-family residence (and in some cases a townhouse), you will contribute to an escrow account for *homeowners' insurance*. (In some cases you can pre-pay your annual homeowners' insurance instead of contributing to an escrow account.) Most lenders will require you to pay one full year of insurance before the loan closes.

If you are buying a condominium, the entire development will have a homeowners' association to govern and maintain the property. The association will be required to have a master insurance policy, which means that you do not have to pay homeowners' insurance.

However, the association will require that you pay a monthly *assessment fee* to cover the common-area tasks (exterior building maintenance and repair, landscaping, grounds maintenance, snow shoveling, etc.). You make this payment directly to the homeowners' association as a separate payment from your mortgage payment.

Private Mortgage Insurance (Pmi)

In the years before so many creative mortgage options became available, lenders expected home buyers to make a down payment of 20 percent of the purchase price and borrow the remaining 80 percent of the property value through a mortgage loan. If a buyer did not have a 20 percent down payment, they couldn't get a mortgage and couldn't buy a house.

Companies recognized a market need and created risk management programs that now allow borrowers to put down less than 20 percent. This insurance product is called *private mortgage insurance (PMI)*. The insurance company insures the difference between 80 percent of the purchase price of the house and the percentage down payment the borrower is able to make. For example, if a borrower puts down 15 percent, the mortgage insurance company would insure the remaining 5 percent (above the 80 percent loan amount) of the purchase price of the home. Borrowers will make an additional payment as part of their total mortgage payment for PMI. The amount of the monthly premium depends on the kind of mortgage program (fixed rate or adjustable rate) as well as the percentage of down payment. The mortgage insurance premium will be higher with a lower down payment

PMI gets a bad name. Many people think of it as a rip-off that no borrower should ever accept, but this isn't necessarily true.

PMI is not permanent. For some borrowers, paying PMI for a few years is the only option for buying a house. For others, there are other ways to structure loans (for example, using second mortgages, which have their own set of pros and cons) to avoid paying PMI.

The point is that if you plan to make a down payment that is less than 20 percent, don't automatically dismiss PMI. Talk to your loan officer to learn about the pros and cons. If it's a choice between paying your landlord another year's worth of rent and beginning to build equity in your own home, PMI might be a reasonable alternative.

SAILING YOUR BOAT

The *Titanic* sank because people did not pay attention to warnings about the icebergs. There are plenty of icebergs waiting for the uninformed buyer, and the largest of these, the one that can sink your dreams of buying a home, waits at the beginning of the process: discovering that you can't get the loan you thought you could after you've already signed a purchase contract on a house.

How can you avoid this disaster? It's straightforward and easy. Obtain a pre-approval for your loan before you visit your first open house.

Being pre-approved is the most important step in obtaining a loan. Too many people assume that they can afford and qualify for a certain priced home before they understand all the facts. They go out with their realtor, find a house, write a contract, and *then* start talking to a loan officer, only to find out that either the payment is going to be too high or they are not qualified for the type of loan that they need. If they have given the seller earnest money (good faith money to take the house temporarily off the market), there are no guarantees that they will get the money back.

ANYONE CAN WRITE A PRE-APPROVAL

Here's another iceberg. Any loan officer can write a pre-approval letter without verifying any information about the borrower. If a pre-approval is written without a thorough review of the borrower's financial situation, the pre-approval is worth less than the paper it's written on. A pre-approval doesn't mean that you will get a loan.

Many real estate agents have been burned and are apprehensive of both pre-qualification and pre-approval letters, because they have seen too many deals fall through due to faulty or truly unqualified pre-approvals. In fact, a smart real estate agent will not take a borrower out to see a house without a pre-approval and will call the loan officer to ensure that the right steps have been taken in pre-approving the borrower. It is only a piece of paper, and most smart agents are less interested in the paper than in the legitimacy of the words on the paper.

AVOIDING ICEBERGS

The borrower controls his or her destiny. If you want a pre-approval to serve you as a real tool in obtaining a house you can afford and a mortgage that suits your financial situation and your needs, take an hour to meet with your loan officer. He should examine the documents that verify your financial situation (more about this later). This information tells him what he needs to know to pre-approve you for a loan and to identify and discuss the kinds of programs that will be available.

When you find a home and actually commit to a mortgage, an underwriter will match your qualifications (as proven by the personal documentation that you will provide) to the loan program guidelines. If you qualify for each guideline, the underwriter will approve the loan. Based on that approval, the lender will give you the money to buy the home.

During a reputable pre-approval consultation, your loan officer will examine the same documents that the underwriter will review. The loan officer operates under the same guidelines that the underwriter will use, matching your qualification with various mortgage program requirements so that you will know how much money you can borrow and under what terms before you have looked at even one property.

If the loan officer knows the mortgage program guidelines, and you have properly satisfied those guidelines, you can walk out of the meeting feeling comfortable and confident in looking for a home.

If you are working with a real estate agent, he or she will love the fact that you and your loan officer have been thorough and have taken this step to prove you are a legitimate buyer. Your realtor will have much more leverage in making an offer to a seller on your behalf because she knows that you will be able to obtain a mortgage to buy the home.

Isn't it Enough to be Pre-qualified?

The short answer is no. A pre-qualification is often confused with a pre-approval. A pre-qualification usually only requires a loan officer to obtain a quick credit report and ask the borrower's income. Based on these two factors, the loan officer will assume that the borrower is qualified and write a pre-qualification letter. A full pre-approval, however, requires paperwork and verification of all the relevant information.

What if, for example, the borrower inadvertently gives the loan officer incorrect information? Mistakes and misrepresentations happen all the time. If the loan officer does not personally review every single document that is required, the borrower is sailing toward a very large block of ice.

Though it is the loan officer's responsibility to know the programs and to know how to pre-approve a borrower, it is the borrower's responsibility to choose a loan officer who will take the steps that result in an eventual loan approval. If your loan officer does not ask for all the documents required for loan approval, you should question why. Even better, find another loan officer.

Pre-underwriting: It's All In The Software

Many buyers are under the impression that an underwriter manually tallies the numbers, analyzing and calculating, until voilà—we have an approval. Not too long ago this was correct. Now, as you can imagine, we have software that automatically analyzes all the relevant information and "underwrites" the loan.

It is a great tool and has improved the pre-approval process. Think about it. Once the borrower has given all the important information to the loan officer—rather, once the loan officer has asked all the relevant and important questions—the loan officer will enter that information into the application on her computer and import that application form as well as the credit report into the underwriting software.

Within thirty seconds the software has underwritten the loan. As long as the loan officer has entered the information correctly, and the loan is approved by the automated underwriting software program, it will be approved by the "real" underwriter. The underwriter's job, then, is to verify the information on the application and on the underwriting software report, verify the appraisal as compared to the purchase price, and verify the borrower's documents (that everything is legitimate and accurate). The underwriter is the final check to protect the lender's money.

THERE'S SO MUCH PAPERWORK

Without the documentation to verify the borrower's qualifications, a loan officer cannot realistically and ethically promise an underwriter's approval. Sometimes people tell me that they cannot find their documents, that they just do not have the time to look for the documents, or that they will provide the required information when they find a house and are actually ready to commit to a loan.

Unfortunately, it does take some time to gather and sort the documents needed to qualify for a mortgage, but in order to get a full pre-approval this is a valuable and necessary investment of your time. Your loan officer should be proactive in helping you understand which documents will work. Not everyone is organized to the point of saving every bill, pay stub, or asset statement. Your loan officer can help you identify alternate documents. Also, if you cannot or do not want to provide these documents, there are programs (that I will discuss later) that do not require documentation.

In the end, though, it is the borrower's responsibility to locate, organize, and bring the documents to the pre-approval consultation with the loan officer.

Do I Need My Birth Certificate?

During a consultation with a client with whom I already had done several loans, he moaned about the pain of locating all his documents, "I'm just glad that you didn't need my birth certificate," he said sarcastically. I replied, trying to hold back a smile, "You mean you didn't bring it?"

He stopped shuffling his documents and looked up completely frustrated until I couldn't hold my smile any longer. Yes, for some people finding documents can be painful, but, again—no documentation, no loan approval.

So Exactly What Paperwork Do I Need?

You must document any assets or income that you want considered as qualification for your mortgage. In general, count on needing the three essential categories of documentation: pay stubs, tax returns, and asset statements. If there is more than one borrower, this documentation must be included for both.

Additionally, all borrowers will be asked to provide statements about their debts—the amount of money they owe and the required monthly payments.

Paystubs: Thirty days' worth of pay stubs should suffice unless you have recently changed jobs. Then the requirements might be different.

The pay stubs should have your name, the company's name and address, and a breakdown of your full pay, including a year-to-date summary. If you receive bonus, commission, vacation, overtime, or any other nonregular income, it must appear on the pay stubs. If you have multiple jobs and want all sources of income considered, bring pay stubs for each job.

Tax Returns: In general, one year of full tax returns that includes all W-2 statements will be required. A self-employed borrower will need to bring two years of full personal returns and sometimes even business financials.

Asset Statements: For any liquid asset account—checking, savings, stock, or retirement (IRA, 401-K, etc.)—you will need to have at least two consecutive months of statements. The statements must be official documents from the institution that holds the funds. If you use online printouts, these documents must have your name, address, account number, and a full record of each account. Further, you'll need all the numbered pages, in order, even if the last pages are blank or seem to have "irrelevant" information. (If the first page says 1 of 5, then you need to produce all 5 pages.)

Be aware that many online printouts cannot be used as they do not present all the information required. You may need to contact the institution that holds your assets and ask them to provide you with a statement that does contain the required information. This can add time to your process, and so it's another example of where you, the borrower, can benefit from asking the loan officer's advice up front.

Liabilities And Debts: If a borrower currently owns one or more properties with mortgages, lines of credit, or other liens, the underwriter requires documents that verify other mortgage payments and tax and insurance payments. If the property is a rental property, you will need lease or rental agreements.

THE PAPERWORK BRIDGE

The whole point of providing documentation is to build a case for a strong and legitimate loan approval. By providing all the documents in the beginning, you are starting to build one side of a bridge; the other side will be the loan approval. The risk of this bridge collapsing is in your lack of documentation and the loan officer's inability to find a suitable loan program.

Chapter 2:
Selecting A Loan Officer

The Process Begins With The
Most Important Step

Every day in this country someone closes on the purchase of a new home. Thousands of buyers march into a title company with their real estate agent (usually), attorney (sometimes), and loan officer (rarely) to complete a process that started weeks or months earlier.

The television and Internet ads make it look so simple. Prospective buyers find the perfect home at the perfect price. They call (shop) around for the best interest rate, get pre-qualified for a mortgage, and in less than a month take proud possession of their new home. A lot of people do this all the time, right? It's a short, simple, and pain-free process, right? All you need to find is the best interest rate, right?

Not necessarily. In fact, I meet people every week whose experience in getting a mortgage is just the opposite. Instead of a smooth ride, their experience is harrowing, frustrating, and full of surprises, delays, and unexpected expenses.

So how do you make your home buying experience a happily-ever-after story instead of a horror show? By choosing a team of industry professionals you like and trust.

START WITH THE BEST LOAN OFFICER
YOU CAN FIND

The single biggest home-buyer mistake is in making a mortgage decision based strictly on interest rate—especially if it's a teaser interest rate quoted over the phone. Choosing a mortgage is not like buying a bottle of bleach: one mortgage lender's products and services are not just like the next lender's offerings. Whether you are a first-time home-buyer or an experienced buyer who has purchased a home before, the key to figuring out this puzzle is to find a great loan officer and then put that person to work for you.

Why? Because the loan officer, more than any other individual in the home-buying process, is the person whom the home buyer depends on most. If you don't get a mortgage, you can't buy a house. You can shop for houses. You can even bid on one and sign a contract to buy. But if there are problems in the mortgage approval process, you can end up paying more money than you expected or even losing the house you wanted to buy.

While there are many aspects of purchasing a house and securing a mortgage that are completely beyond your control, identifying and doing business with an outstanding loan officer rests entirely in your hands.

WHY IS THE LOAN OFFICER SO
IMPORTANT?

A loan officer pulls together a pile of paperwork and quotes some interest rates. What's the big deal?

Borrowing the money to buy a house represents one of the biggest commitments (after bungee jumping!) that you are ever likely to make. As with any other big decision, a borrower will benefit from the professional guidance of an expert who has your interest at heart.

In leading you through the not-so-simple process of securing a mortgage, it's the loan officer's job to understand your goals in buying a home, to analyze the details of your financial situation—debts, assets, earnings, and risk, to research the optimal loan programs for you, to explain and compare those programs, and to secure the mortgage that matches your needs.

Today there is no such thing as an easy, straightforward, one-size-fits-all loan. A good loan officer's job requires concentration, analytical skills, integrity, and discipline. No matter what you hear or read, obtaining a mortgage is not simple and almost never entirely pain-free.

WHAT EXACTLY DOES A LOAN OFFICER DO?

A loan officer's first responsibility is to listen, really listen, to the borrower. In any good, solid relationship, things go well because people communicate; a great loan officer has superb listening skills.

Second, an effective loan officer will educate his or her clients, explaining any new or unfamiliar terms relating to the details of the various loan programs.

After finding the loan program that best satisfies the borrower's needs, the loan officer verifies that the borrower can satisfy each of the loan program requirements. It is essential to understand that every loan program has (usually) more than a dozen main requirements, and if the borrower cannot satisfy even one of those, the loan may be denied.

Third, once the loan officer has a program that matches the borrower's qualifications, she must collect the relevant documentation that will verify these qualifications.

Fourth, the loan officer ensures that the loan process goes smoothly and the loan closes. When a borrower buys a house there are many people and business entities (in addition to the borrower and lender) involved in the transaction: the sellers, real estate agents, attorneys, condo associations, insurance agents, inspectors, appraisers, as well as a few others. A top-notch loan officer can supply the glue that holds all these special interests together.

THE DIFFERENT TYPES OF MORTGAGE LENDERS

There are many lenders in the marketplace. Most of them are one of three types: banker, mortgage broker, or mortgage banker. Regardless of the entity, the representatives who deal directly with the borrower are typically called loan officers. However, the scope of their responsibilities varies greatly depending on whom they represent.

A banker works for a depository institution with money in its vaults. Some banks choose to put that money to work by making home mortgage loans. The nice thing about a bank is that they make their own rules. Banks conduct their own risk assessment, do their underwriting in-house (as opposed to literally mailing the borrower's file to another office in another city or even state), and approve and fund loans themselves. If they decide that they want to make a loan, they have the money and authority to do exactly that. The downside is that banks are generally conservative, and while they may make mortgage loans for their best customers or high net-worth individuals, they generally have limited mortgage loan programs available.

If you are an important or long-term client of a local bank, that institution may be delighted to offer you a mortgage loan with very competitive terms. Ask them. However, if you are a regular Joe or Jane, need a customized loan, or have risk factors (which we will discuss later), many banks may not be interested in loaning you money at all, or if they do it may be at a premium that may not be competitive with other options in the marketplace.

The second type of lender is a mortgage broker. Mortgage

brokers are individuals or companies that represent various lenders, such as institutional banks. Brokers do not have the money to fund loans; rather they serve as the salesperson for the mortgage programs that these money sources make available to them.

Brokers work at the front end of the loan process. A broker's job is to pursue leads, collect potential borrower's information, and match that borrower to the program that fits best. Once the borrower commits to a loan, the broker hands him, his paperwork, and the responsibility for the balance of the loan processing to the lender.

A mortgage banker falls between a bank and a broker. A mortgage banker understands a borrower's needs and finances, matches those to the optimal loan program from a wide range of programs, and then manages that loan from application through the closing on the borrower's new home.

Mortgage banks have giant credit lines that enable them to borrow money temporarily to fund the borrower's loan. After closing, the mortgage bank then immediately "sells" the loan to the ultimate lender (called the end-lender), who will service the loan (i.e., send the borrower their monthly mortgage invoice and receive and process the corresponding payment).

AND THE RIGHT CHOICE IS?

For borrowers who have a special or preferred relationship with their local bank, that may be a place to start. However, most people do not have such a relationship, and, for most of us, that means loan officers who are mortgage brokers and mortgage bankers typically offer more loan types and programs at competitive rates, regardless of the borrower's qualifications.

The service trade-off between a loan officer who is a broker as opposed to a loan officer who is a mortgage banker is that the borrower deals with a broker on the front end of the process, but once the borrower commits to a loan, the broker's involvement ends, she goes away, and someone else is responsible for getting the rest of the process completed. If you are confused by the title someone gives you, ask them who you will be dealing with once you commit to a loan, who do you contact if you have questions, and most important, who do you call when there's a problem, whether large or small.

The loan officer, who represents the mortgage bank, works with the borrower all the way through the process, from the day you first call to meet with them until the day you push back from the closing table with the keys to your new home. Loan officers who represent mortgage banks are a one-stop start-to-finsh source of expertise and assistance.

You may think you don't care whether the broker or someone else is doing the processing work on your loan, just as long as everything is completed correctly and on time. And let me repeat those words: *completed correctly and on time.* This does not always happen.

Here's an analogy. Let's say you are having some pipe problems with your kitchen sink. You talk to a few friends and get a few referrals. Plumber #1 comes to the house, examines the situation, gives you a quote, and then tells you that he just writes the orders; he will have to subcontract out the actual work. The subcontracted plumber will complete the work, and if there are any problems with the quality or timeliness of the work, you will have to take it up with the subcontracted plumber.

Plumber #2 examines the job, provides a quote (at the same rates and terms as Plumber #1), but commits that he personally will do every bit of the work and will take responsibility for resolving any problems that occur. Which plumber would you choose?

LICENSING REQUIREMENTS FOR A LOAN OFFICER

Loan officer licensing requirements vary from state to state. Check with your state to see if loan officers are required to be certified and licensed. If they are, ask to see your loan officer's certification or license. If he does not have this documentation, check with the city or state organization that is responsible for mortgage lending laws to see if the loan officer is in fact licensed. If not, find another loan officer.

THE CHOICE IS NOT OBVIOUS

Choose a loan officer who is willing to meet you in person, answer your questions, and take your telephone calls. Seek the person who explains the various mortgage options in a clear and honest way, invests their time to understand your short- and long-term financial goals, and talks to you and your spouse or partner about your needs and desires in buying a home.

The loan officer who wants to spend time with you, get to know you, and consult with you about your personal and financial goals is more focused on satisfying you as a client than on what she has to gain from the loan transaction.

The main focus should be on you, the borrower. You want to be happy on the day that you close on your new house—not stressed because the loan process went poorly or was delayed. So when you meet with a loan officer, try to get a sense that her priority is to make you happy. Get to know the person before you decide to do business with her.

HERE ARE SOME QUESTIONS
TO GET YOU STARTED.

- Request names and phone numbers of references from a few years ago and a few months ago, from borrowers, real estate agents, lawyers, and other sources.

- Ask how long they have been responsible for originating loans.

- Ask how long the company has been doing business.
- Are they licensed?
- What do they like about what they do?
- Why should you work with them rather than another loan officer?

The process by which you choose the person who will assist you in deciding on the right loan program takes time and patience. Like choosing any other professional, you will want to be detailed and thorough. It is easy to compare one loan officer's closing costs and interest rates. It's not so easy to compare their commitment to their clients' satisfaction and happiness.

I cannot stress the importance of choosing the right loan officer. Base that decision on the loan officer's experience, qualifications, references, and personality, and *then* compare mortgage terms, closing costs, and rates. In truth, on any given day, interest rates from most mortgage lenders basically will be the same because, in general, most lenders base their rates on the same sources (their lenders).

So, yes obtaining the best interest rate is an important consideration in any mortgage process. If you invest the time up front to choose a well-qualified and client-oriented loan officer, most of the time that person can secure a loan at an interest rate that is competitive while providing premium client service. This, in the end, will make you a happy homeowner.

CHAPTER 3:
IT'S ALL ABOUT RISK
(NOT ABOUT RATE)

Strong borrowers—less risky borrowers—are those who show a history of doing all the right things. A strong borrower has paid bills on time, has not accumulated significant debt, has saved money, and has maintained steady employment.

The borrower's risk factor determines the programs that are available as well as the interest rate.

Consider two borrowers. Borrower #1 has paid her rent and all other bills on time, has a 20 percent down payment, another $50,000 in the bank, a high credit score, and long-time employment with the same company. Borrower #2 paid his rent late three times in the last twelve months, has a 5 percent down payment, $5,000 in the bank, a low credit score, and has changed jobs three times in the last two years. Who do you think is a higher risk? To which borrower do you think a lender would rather loan money? And if you were a lender, would you be willing to offer them an identical interest rate?

A borrower who has not shown satisfactory history in any or all of these areas would, you might say, make a lender more nervous. When a lender reviews a file that is risky, they have the same thoughts that you or I would have. "Well, this person has been late here, and here, and here, and hasn't saved much money, and has $10,000 in credit card debt. How do I know he is going to be able to make the mortgage payment on time? I'm going to have to cover my risk, and so I will have to charge a higher interest rate, if I agree to make this risky person a loan."

Here is one of the great mortgage truths: *The more certain the lender is that the borrower will make the mortgage payment, month after month, right on time, the more likely it is that the borrower will be offered the most attractive mortgage programs and best interest rates.*

ALL FIXED RATES ARE NOT THE SAME

As a mortgage professional, my favorite question comes from the person who is shopping around for the best rate. The phone rings, and the conversation goes something like this.

"Hello. I am buying a home and got your name from someone at work. I'd like to know what your best 30-year fixed rate is today."

"Well, that depends. Have you paid your rent on time, not accumulated a lot of debt, saved money, and maintained steady employment?"

Hopefully you see my point. If interest rates are based on risk, there cannot be a universal rate for everyone. Different lenders have different programs for different borrowers.

Pure and simple, lenders make money from the interest they charge, and if a borrower shows any potential risk for making late payments or not making payments at all, the lender will charge a higher interest rate to ensure they make their profit in the early years of the transaction, before any issues develop with the borrower. Obviously, just because a borrower has a less than perfect history does not mean that he will have a rocky mortgage history; however, lenders base their assessment of risk on history, which is the only data available.

The same philosophy pertains to programs as it does for rates, which means that certain mortgage programs will not be offered to all borrowers. Less risky borrowers will have more programs available to them. A borrower who has a great history and wants to put only 5 percent down—a fairly risky loan—may be offered that type of program, whereas someone with poor history may not be able to secure a mortgage without putting a higher percentage down.

The important thing to remember is that every borrower has a personal, unique situation and history, and it is impossible and even irresponsible for a loan officer to offer programs and rates without knowing the borrower's financial history.

INSIDE AND OUTSIDE THE BOX PART 1

A borrower who is a very low-risk borrower is (a term I prefer) an In-The-Box borrower. Someone in this situation is making a 20 percent down payment, has at least a 720 credit score, a debt-to-income (DTI) ratio of no higher than 38 percent, and has at least six months' cash reserves, which is enough money to cover their committed expenses for half a year.

In-The-Box

780 Credit Score	20% Down Payment
6 Months' Reserves	Owner Occupied
33% DTI	Single Family

These factors can be complicated, and the loan officer needs to make sure that the borrower can satisfy each guideline (risk factor) to qualify for a certain loan program. If any of these factors fall outside the box, then the programs and interest rates may be different.

Big Picture/Little Picture

When you meet with your loan officer, your portfolio of documents in hand, he will consider the various risk factors that will determine both your program and rate eligibility. The loan officer will consider the overall file and each individual factor. A borrower may have a mostly solid file, but even one sub-par risk factor can cause a problem.

For example, a borrower may have great savings, a high income, and 25 percent down payment, but poor credit scores to the point that certain programs may not be available. A different borrower may have excellent credit scores and history, high balances in their savings accounts, but cannot verify enough income to qualify for the loan program they want.

Many times the borrower feels that his big picture is great but may not realize that an individual risk factor can still cause a problem. The good news is that there are programs available that will accept borrowers with any or even all high risk factors. Interest rates will be higher than they are for borrowers with lower risk, but there are creative ways that people with high-risk profiles can still get a mortgage to purchase a home. Here are the main risk factors.

Credit scoring is the most important risk factor. The Fair Isaacs Corporation (FICO) is the established and accepted system for incorporating a person's credit history (payment patterns) into a credit report and assigning the individual a credit score.

The three main credit repositories—Equifax, Trans Union, and Experian—collect and report this history on practically anyone with a Social Security number. The data incorporates payments on credit cards, automobile payments, student loans, and, most important, mortgages. The Fair Isaacs credit report will aggregate the three reports from these bureaus to create credit scores used to evaluate the strength of the borrower.

Most of the time, the three credit bureaus produce different credit scores because they calculate scores in slightly different ways. However, assuming they have the same information to evaluate the credit history, the bureaus should report about the same scores, usually twenty points or less apart. Sometimes, however, the scores vary by more than twenty points. This can occur when one of the bureaus has received negative (derogatory) credit history for some item (like a late credit card payment or even a late utility bill payment) that the other bureaus did not receive.

Open credit issues can be resolved (and this is usually required by the lender before the loan closes). The borrower can contact the creditor that reported the problem and pay the amount due. If the item was reported in error, the borrower can request that the creditor report the correct history to the bureau. This process may take thirty to sixty days and another thirty to ninety days for the credit report to reflect the change and result in an improved credit score.

Credit scoring is critical for a loan approval, and you should resolve any credit issues immediately. Do not wait until you decide to buy a house to view your credit reports and correct any errors.

WHERE DO I STAND?

Credit scores are the driving risk factor in determining loan eligibility. As you can see, the higher your score, the lower the lender's perceived risk.

Excellent	800
Very Good	760
Good	720
OK	680
Poor	620
Very Poor	500

Your credit reports will show credit card debt, on-time/ delinquent payment history, delinquencies and defaults (collections, liens, foreclosures), and mortgage history. Any late payments will lower the overall score. For example, one late mortgage payment can lower your score by sixty points.

People who make their payments on time, keep their debt balances low, and do not own an unnecessary number of credit cards and/or other debt should have good scores.

Clients often ask my advice on what they can do with credit cards to either maintain or improve their credit scores. There is no simple answer. You do want to show a credit history, so canceling all credit cards is not always the way to go. I recommend using common sense. If you have credit cards that you do not use, cut them up and cancel them. It is always better to use a few cards regularly and make (at least) the minimum payment every single month than to keep ten or more active cards and only use a few of them.

For purposes of your credit score, it is not necessary to pay all your credit cards down to a zero balance. Credit scores are based on the amount of debt per card compared to the amount of available credit per card. If you have ten cards that all show debt up to the maximum available, your credit score will probably suffer. If you have ten cards but only three of them have balances, and these balances are significantly below the maximum allowed, your score may not be affected at all.

In summary, although the credit scoring system is not an exact science, it works pretty well in painting a picture of someone's credit history. People with good credit have good credit scores for a reason.

Income Documentation

As we have seen, *income documentation* is another important element of the pre-approval process. A borrower who states that she makes $40,000 per year will be asked to prove it with current documents that verify the numbers.

Again, the most commonly used documents are pay stubs and/ or tax returns with W-2s.

It is important to know that *bonus income* is treated in a special way. In general, if a borrower received the bonus income in the same year she will receive the loan, the loan officer will calculate monthly bonus income by dividing the bonus amount by twelve. If, however, the borrower will not receive the bonus until after the loan closes, the total bonus amount cannot be used to qualify for the loan. For people who receive *commission income*, there is a similar process.

Self-employed borrowers often receive their income in various forms. In addition, due to various deductions on their tax returns, their actual income is not reflected on the tax returns, which can obviously cause problems in qualifying for a loan.

If a borrower does not earn enough income to qualify for a loan (see Ratio section below) or if their income is undocumented (if they receive a significant portion of their compensation in cash), they may be directed to look at programs that do not require income verification.

In these situations, the loan officer will state the borrower's income on the application, but will not require documentation to verify the amount. This amount must be reasonable for someone in the borrower's line of work. For example, if a borrower is a fifth-grade teacher, he could reasonably say that he makes $40,000 per year, but he could not reasonably say that he makes $400,000 per year because this amount is not reasonable for his field.

In making a no income verification loan, the lender takes a greater risk because the qualification of the loan is based on unverifiable income. The lender will charge a higher interest rate, in some cases, and may require additional terms.

There are also no income verification loan programs where no income amount is listed on the application.

Using our fifth-grade teacher example, let's say that to qualify for a certain loan the teacher would have to report an unreasonable income of $500,000 (an amount no underwriter would accept); we would leave the income box blank on the application. Since there is no income reported, there is no income to prove. However, this borrower represents an even greater risk to the lender, and there must be factors (perhaps a 20 percent down payment or larger personal assets) that offer the lender compensating factors. Still, an underwriter will make a subjective decision if the fifth-grade teacher can afford this house based on other guideline items. So the loan officer, in this case, may want to do a loan where neither income nor assets nor employment are disclosed on the application.

Regardless, the lender views a borrower like this as an even greater risk than someone with undocumented income and will charge a higher compensating interest rate.

Debt-to-income

The next important factor in loan pre-approval is the borrower's *debt-to-income (DTI) ratio*. The loan officer adds the total of the borrower's current monthly obligations (for example, credit card minimum payments, automobile payments, credit union, or student loans) to the total proposed monthly mortgage payment (PITI) plus any applicable homeowners' assessments, and then divides that amount into the borrower's gross monthly income.

For example, if a borrower's monthly total debt is $1,000 and their monthly income amount is $4,000, then the DTI is 25 percent (1,000/4,000 = 25%).

Lenders like to see the DTI no higher than 38 percent, though it is common for loans to be approved with ratios in the 40 to 50 percent range. In fact, I have been able to approve loans for borrowers with DTIs as high as 65 percent! However, the higher the DTI, the higher the risk to the lender, and the more likely this will be reflected in the interest rate or terms of the loan.

Assets And Reserves

The more money you have saved in *liquid asset accounts* (checking, savings, money market, stocks and bonds, IRAs, 401Ks, or other nonrestricted retirement accounts) at the time of application, the more qualified you will be for your loan. All other things being equal, a borrower with $50,000 in assets is a more qualified borrower than someone with only $5,000.

An asset account can be any account where money can be withdrawn to cover your down payment or closing costs. This doesn't mean that you actually have to use this money for the down payment or closing costs; it may be taken into account only to qualify you, whether you do or do not spend it on mortgage-related expenses. As I have stated, the lender will usually require two to three months of consecutive asset statements to verify the balances.

We mentioned *reserves* earlier. To be considered a strong borrower, you should have four to six times your total monthly mortgage payment in an asset account *after you have closed on your home.*

If your PITI (principal, interest, tax, and insurance, plus association dues or homeowners' assessment if applicable) is $2,000, then six times this number is $12,000 in reserves.

Consider this example. A borrower starts the loan process with $20,000 in total assets. Her down payment is $8,000, closing costs are $4,000, and her total mortgage payment (PITI) is $1,400. After closing, she would have $8,000 in her asset accounts, which is slightly less than the six months of reserves (6 × $1400 = $8400) that her lender wants her to have.

The money in these asset accounts must be the borrower's own funds. An underwriter will question and require documentation and an extensive written explanation for any large, unexplained, or unusual deposits. Other than gifts from direct family members, all funds for down payment and/or closing costs must come from the borrower. Generally, a borrower cannot borrow the money to make a down payment or to cover closing costs.

Many people use retirement accounts for reserve requirements. Since most of the time a person would have to pay taxes and a penalty for withdrawing money from these accounts prior to retirement, lenders only allow 70 percent of the total balance in these accounts toward qualifying. If a borrower has an IRA worth $100,000, the loan officer would qualify with only $70,000 of that amount.

Basically the lender wants to make sure that you have "rainy day" money in case something unexpected happens to you or your income. Having said that, there are many programs for people with few or, amazingly, no assets or reserves. Many first-time home-buyer programs have more liberal guidelines so that borrowers aren't required to have a full six months of reserves without being penalized on their interest rate.

As with income documentation, for some borrowers it is not possible to verify assets or reserves. There are programs that, like income documentation, do not require the borrower to verify the asset accounts. In general, as you would guess, the rates may be (and probably will be) somewhat higher.

LOAN TO VALUE (LTV)

Down payment is the amount of money that you put toward the purchase of your house. *The more money you put down, the lower the risk.* It is still a good, old-fashioned loan when borrowers put down 20 percent of the purchase price, and so someone who puts down 10 percent is a higher risk, someone with 5 percent down is an even higher risk, and someone with 0 percent down payment is the highest risk of all, as she is not putting any personal assets into the transaction. The lender is, in effect, absorbing all the risk.

Loan-to-Value (LTV) is the other side of down payment, and it is one of the most important terms, after credit score, that loan officers consider. Whereas down payment details the percentage of the purchase price that the borrower puts into the transaction, LTV refers to the money that the lender puts in—the amount of the loan itself. To find LTV, simply divide the loan amount into the purchase price or property value, whichever is lower. If a borrower is buying a \$100,000 property and puts \$12,000 down, and the loan amount is \$88,000, then the LTV is 88 percent (88,000/100,000 = 88%). Realtors usually concern themselves with down payment amount; lenders focus on LTV.

When a loan officer talks about LTV, he is talking about the amount of risk that the bank is taking to lend money. Again, it is a good, solid (old-fashioned loan) to be at 80 percent LTV. A 90 percent LTV loan is more risky, 95 percent even more risky, and 100 percent LTV is the riskiest.

OCCUPANCY

A home buyer must declare the *occupancy* of the property. The borrower may be going to live in the property as a primary home. They may be purchasing the property as a second home (living there part time) or as an investment (not living there and renting or leasing the property).

From a lender's point of view, the least risky of these occurs when a borrower is buying the property as a primary residence. A lender is more nervous about an investment property where a renter may suddenly pack up and leave for New Zealand to bungee jump, rather than when a borrower is living in the property every day.

The more units a property contains, the higher the risk. If you have a building with four units, and you live in one (of the units) as a primary residence while renting the other three, your lender sees more risk because, once again, your three renters could take off for New Zealand, Tanzania, and Argentina (all beautiful countries with bungee opportunities). Without their rent checks, you may have a serious problem in making your monthly mortgage payment.

If the property is entirely for investment purposes (the owner does not occupy the property), the risk is bigger still.

PROPERTY TYPE

The *type of property* may affect loan availability. Generally, single-family houses carry the least risk, and high-rise condominiums carry the greatest risk. New construction condominiums add even more risk. Many lenders do not want any part of a 200-unit new construction condo complex. The possibility that many of the units will not sell scares them off. If you are interested in this type of property, it is essential that you work with a lender who is capable of financing new construction or condo conversion properties. This is another topic to be sure, and it should be discussed up front with your loan officer.

INSIDE AND OUTSIDE THE BOX PART 2

How the system works should now be clear. The lender has a checklist. If you satisfy the checklist, you will have the widest range of programs with the best interest rates available to you. If, however, you do not satisfy one, some, or all of the items on the list, things change.

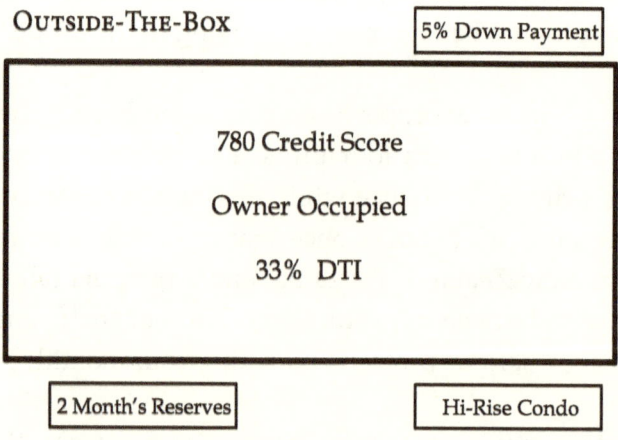

The more outside the box, the fewer programs are available and the higher the rate.

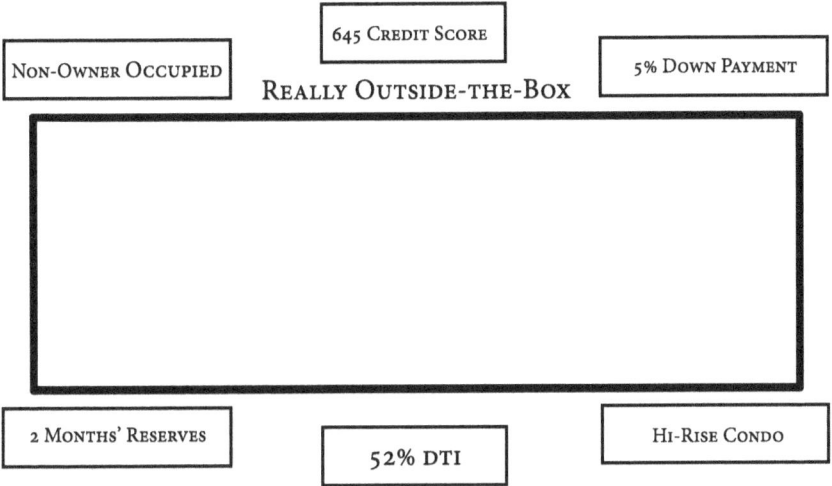

Clearly an empty box is a very high risk loan. Again my purpose here is not to discourage you. There are programs for just about everyone. The loan officer may have to do more research to find programs that will accept certain high risk factors. Recognize that there will be trade-offs in these more risky scenarios.

BALANCING THE RISK

The good news is that with compensating factors the lender may make exceptions to the guidelines. If a borrower has a 635 credit score (on the low side) but is making a 25 percent down payment, has eight months of reserves, five years of employment with the same company, and a DTI of 33 percent, the lender may make an exception for the low credit score.

If another borrower has only $3,000 in assets and wants to do a 100 percent LTV loan (borrowing 100 percent of the purchase price with 0 down payment), but has a credit score of 795 (fabulous) and zero debt, the lender may make an exception and accept the borrower for a standard loan program.

The opposite may be true as well. A borrower may have a credit score of 782—and this is the trap that many people fall into regarding credit score alone—but a DTI of 57 percent, an LTV of 90 percent, and only two months of reserves. The lender may assess this situation as too risky and offer a limited set of mortgage programs at higher interest rates.

Credit score is the king of risk factors but may not be able to overrule the combination of other poor risk factors.

CHAPTER 4:
THE FIXED RATE OR
ADJUSTABLE RATE DILEMMA

There are basically two types of programs—you might even call them payment plans—for the payment of the principal and interest. The first is a *fixed-rate mortgage*, which is the most conservative and popular program.

With a fixed-rate mortgage the loan is amortized (put on an installment payment plan) over a certain number of years; the interest rate never changes, and as a result the payment will never change as well. The most popular program is the 30-year fixed-rate mortgage, though for those who want to pay the loan off faster, there are 25-, 20-, 15-, 10-, and 5-year fixed-rate programs.

Don't get confused by the shorter terms. The shorter term qualifies for a lower interest rate because the lender has the principal and interest repaid faster.

The total amount of interest that you pay over the life of the loan is less with a shorter term, but what borrowers sometimes forget is that since you will be paying the loan off in fewer years, the mortgage payment (PITI) will be larger than if the mortgage was spread over thirty years.

Consider a loan for $150,000 with a 30-year fixed rate at 6.50 percent compared to a 15-year fixed-rate loan for the same loan amount at 6.125 percent. Remember, if a buyer chooses a shorter amortization period, they will be rewarded with a lower interest rate. In this example, the payments would look like this:

30-Year Fixed	15-Year Fixed
$948.10	**$1,275.93**

As the borrower you have a decision to make. Do you want a lower monthly payment in return for paying more interest over the life of the loan? Or will you accept a higher payment over a shorter term with less total interest paid?

If you choose the 30-year program, you will pay $191,316 in interest over the life of the loan; if you choose the 15-year program, you will pay $79,669.20 in interest, more than $100,000 less.

That's a big difference, but you have to be able to make the monthly payments.

You can go the other way, too. There are even 40- and 50-year programs out there today. Again, the main idea is that with a fixed-rate mortgage, the rate and payment are fixed for the full term of the loan. They will never change.

LEND ME AN ARM

Adjustable-rate mortgages (ARMs) are another commonly available set of loan programs. Like every other mortgage option, they have advantages and disadvantages.

All other things being equal, adjustable-rate programs have lower interest rates than fixed mortgages. With a 5-year ARM, the amortization period will still be thirty years, but the rate and payment will be the same (fixed) only for the first five years of the loan.

At the beginning of the sixth year, the rate adjusts up or down, depending on current prevailing market interest rates, and the rate will then adjust annually for the remainder of the loan. In choosing an ARM you are rolling the dice. Since no one knows where the market is going to be in five years—if I could know that I would be writing a different book—anyone choosing an ARM must give serious consideration to the potential rate adjustments before they commit to a variable-rate loan program.

Lenders offer a range of fixed periods, most commonly 3-, 5-, 7-, and 10-year ARMs. The shorter the fixed-period term, the lower the rate will be. The programs do usually have "caps" (ceilings) for the maximum amount that the rates can adjust over the life of the loan, and so the borrower does have some protection.

BACK TO THE DILEMMA, PLEASE

OK, so what is the best program?

My standard answer: it depends.

Consider this scenario. You are buying a home for $200,000 with a $50,000 down payment. Compare a 30-year fixed rate with an interest rate of 6.50 percent with a 5-year ARM with a rate of 6.00 percent:

30-Year Fixed	5-Year ARM
$948.10	$899.33

A monthly savings of $48.77. Which program do you choose? Here's the question I would ask: Is it more important to have the security that your rate and thus your payment will *never* change, or is it more important to have a lower monthly payment up front in return for dealing with a higher payment when the adjustment periods begin?

How do you feel about this decision? Yes, it is important to look at this intellectually and logically (as a financial planning approach), but you have to live with this payment and sleep at night. Low payments with little sleep are not a good thing. In my opinion either option is fine, but I am not making a borrower's payment. It is essential to decide what program works for you.

However, what if the rate on the ARM is 5.25 percent? Your

payment then will be $828.30, and the monthly difference now is $119.79. That's $1,437.53 a year and $7,187.66 over five years.

If you know that this is a first home, and you will be there for no more than three years, then an ARM may be appropriate. If you are not sure how long you will be in the home, then, again, you have a decision to make.

Remember that whatever program you choose, you can always refinance (where you pay off or replace your current loan with a new one). If you get to the five-year adjustment point and the market is down from the original rate, you can certainly refinance into a new 5-year ARM or even a fixed-rate program. But if you get to the five-year adjustment period and rates are up, you will be stuck with a larger monthly obligation.

THIS IS *INTERESTING*

There are some other options worth mentioning. Recently, interest-only payments have become popular. With these loans, the borrower pays only the interest every month with no money being applied to the principal.

In the first three years of a 30-year mortgage, a very small portion of your monthly payment goes toward reducing principal. Borrowers pay about 1.5 percent to 2.0 percent of the principal annually.

Using our earlier example, if principal and interest payment is $828.30, then the interest portion is $656.25, and the principal portion is $172.05. So your first-year principal reduction is $2,064.60, which is 1.3 percent of your original principal (loan amount). Lenders came up with the idea that since the principal is, initially, such a small amount and housing appreciation in most markets has been so strong, and people do not live in homes now for more than 3 to 5 years, borrowers don't care so much about paying down the principal; they just want to participate in the increasing equity of the property. So lenders came up with interest-only mortgages.

Interest-only mortgages are not for everyone. In obtaining a mortgage the borrower takes on substantial debt, and some people do not like the idea of not paying off their debt. However, with an interest-only program a disciplined borrower can always *choose* to pay principal in addition to the interest at any time and thus have greater flexibility than with a fixed-rate mortgage that requires both principal and interest to be paid every month.

What's my opinion? You guessed it—it depends. Every borrower must assess what makes him or her comfortable.

There is, however, quite a bit of difference in the payment from program to program, depending on the loan amount. Rates for interest only ARMs are usually .125 to .25 percent higher than the principal and interest programs. Here is how a $150,000 principal and interest ARM at 6.00 percent compares to an interest-only ARM at 6.25 percent:

5-Year ARM	5-Year ARM IO
$948.10	**$781.25**

A difference of $47.05. Once again, you have the option of a higher payment where you are paying down principal and will own more of the property when you sell it, or a lower payment with less money out of pocket, where you will owe the exact same amount as when you purchased the property.

If you keep the house for five years and then sell it, with a principal and interest loan (of $150,000) you will have paid down about 8.00 percent of the loan (about $12,000). Or, another way to look at, you are keeping that $12,000 in your pocket to use for furniture, fix ups, or just to keep as a rainy-day fund.

Now we have a "best-of-both-worlds" mortgage program—a 30-year fixed-rate with an initial interest-only period for the first ten years. For people who are nervous about the rate adjusting but like the interest-only option, this is an interesting alternative.

Getting Really Aggressive

For borrowers who like the interest-only programs or want to keep the payment as low as possible, something that people who buy investment properties usually desire, there are some aggressive ARMs. For example, there are 6-month or 1-year ARMs. The rates are even lower than traditional ARMS, but they will adjust sooner and more frequently. In addition, there are ARMS that will adjust monthly. These programs are not for the faint of heart but rather are tools for those who are using properties more for investments than as a home.

My Advice (Seriously)

Let's take a break to consider one very important question that you should not and cannot avoid. *What do you want to spend every month for your total mortgage payment?* Only you can determine the amount that will let you live comfortably and get the sleep you need every night.

If you don't honestly know the answer to this question, don't go further because this is a sign that you are not really ready to buy a home.

However, if you can write down that number—as well as the other numbers for a full budget—you are ready to find a highly qualified loan officer and let him or her help you get started finding the loan program that fits your needs.

Pre-underwriting equals pre-approval equals closing

Now let us go back to recap everything we've covered so far.

If you go to a loan officer who reviews your credit report and qualifying documents, completes an automated underwriting summary, and discusses your financial goals and dreams (and thus has consulted with you about the best ways to structure your loan and the available programs), don't you think this is truly the best scenario for obtaining a mortgage? *A true pre-approval really incorporates all of the above.* A loan officer who serves you as I have described above can write a truly legitimate pre-approval. Anything less is insufficient and meaningless.

SIGNING UP

At the initial consultation, the loan officer will review all qualifying materials with the borrower—including the credit report, the borrower's verification documents, and the borrower's pre-underwriting results. The loan officer will also discuss and review the borrower's *mortgage application* and the resulting *Good Faith Estimate*. Once the loan officer has discussed and explained those documents, and the borrower has signed them as well as certain disclosures, then the borrower is prepared to look for a house and the loan officer is ready to process the loan.

The mortgage application consists of three to four pages of personal information. This document provides the lender with all the information about the borrower that will be considered for underwriting. Basic information like name, current address, marital status, employment history, income, and assets gives the underwriter the information that will be required to evaluate the loan.

The Good Faith Estimate (GFE) is a best-guess estimate of the borrower's closing costs—fees associated with getting the mortgage and buying the property that the borrower will be required to pay at closing.

The most common categories of costs are title insurance, lender fees, appraisal fees, government fees, tax and insurance escrows, and prepaid interest. The loan officer will enter the estimated costs for each of the main sections on the GFE, using her experience of local costs to estimate these fees.

Generally, for purchases, the only fees that the loan officer knows up front are the lender costs. This is the main point of having—no, insisting—the loan officer review the GFE with you. It is by far the most important document that a borrower will sign because it establishes the lender's costs up front.

The loan officer will know the lender costs right from the beginning. The only way that those numbers should change is if the borrower has misrepresented information and the loan officer needs to change programs, or if the loan officer has failed to approve the borrower for the correct program. If for any reason the loan officer needs to change numbers on the GFE, the borrower should get a new GFE to review and sign.

Once the borrower has reviewed the GFE and signs it (verifying that he understands everything), the loan officer cannot add any fees without the borrower's written permission. So if the lender changes the costs any time between the application and the closing—especially at the closing—the borrower has the right to stop and even cancel the transaction.

Sometimes additional costs are required. For example, if a borrower is buying a new construction condominium, and an additional, follow-up appraisal is required to verify that all construction is complete, there may be an additional cost for that appraisal. The loan officer should get permission in writing from the borrower that this additional cost can be added to the GFE and/or settlement statement at the closing.

The rest of the GFE is only an estimate, though it should be an informed estimate based on local costs and the loan officer's recent experience with other transactions. An excellent loan officer should pretty much know what the costs are going to be, although remember that all non-lender costs are estimates and will not be exact. For example, in some states the seller's attorney often chooses the title company. The loan officer does not know which title company the attorney will choose, at the time of application, so title fees will vary from the estimates.

As you can imagine, this part of the application requires trust and attention. The borrower must trust that the loan officer knows the borrower's numbers regarding the estimated closing costs—and that those numbers are not over- or underestimated too much.

Too often these numbers are underestimated, and borrowers are required to bring more money to the closing than they expected or were told to bring. For this reason, the borrower needs to focus on what the loan officer says regarding the closing costs on the GFE and must be willing to ask tough questions about the assumptions on which these costs are based. Now is not the time to daydream about the home that is just around the corner.

FULL DISCLOSURE

In addition to presenting you the application and GFE, the loan officer will review a set of disclosures for you to sign. You will be asked to re-sign many of these again at closing.

In essence, these disclosures are FYI documents meant both to guide and to protect the borrower. Some of them are easier to understand than others. For example, one disclosure verifies that the lender has reviewed your credit report with you (pretty clear). Another asks if you will escrow for taxes and/or insurance premiums (even less clear, as you may not know how or when to declare your intentions for escrowing).

There are certain federal disclosures and certain state disclosures, and so each lender is going to have some variation as to the number of disclosures.

The main point is not to be intimidated by these documents, and if any part of any of the disclosures is unclear, ask the loan officer to explain. When I review these documents I can usually tell if someone is getting nervous or confused, and I will ask them if they understand everything or if I need to review something.

Sometimes, I am sure, there are people who are nervous or confused and do not say anything. It is essential to speak up and ask questions.

SIGNING YOUR LIFE AWAY?

People often ask me what it "means" if they sign the application and GFE. "Have I signed my life away? Can I stop the process? Do I have to buy a home now?" The answers are no, yes, and no.

First (in reverse order), if you are not committed to finding and buying a home, don't sign anything. You should be committed to buying a home before you show up for an application. There is no reason to go through this process unless you are intent on buying a house.

People wrestle in their own minds about whether to buy a home. "Should I buy? Yes, I want to own a house. No, it's too much of a burden. Yes, I want to be able to paint the walls black and pink and not ask my landlord. No, I don't want to pay for new windows." Hopefully you see my point. The signing of the documents should really confirm your decision for yourself, and once you have reviewed all the information with your loan officer, there should be nothing to it.

Once you have signed the application and GFE, you can decide at any time not to buy a home. Never feel that you are chained to this process just because you have taken some steps. Sometimes, after people have decided to buy a home and signed the application, they go home and think about things and then decide to stay where they are for an indefinite period, and this is perfectly fine.

There is no such thing as signing your life away. Not to get too philosophical, but I believe that life is full of change, and that most of the time we have the control as to how our lives change. So, going back to the previous point, you can decide to sign a document, and you can decide to call your loan officer and tell her that you have decided to hold off buying. It's that simple.

Preparing to Look for a Home ... Finally

Now you are ready to look for a house, and you should be proud of yourself. You have completed the most detailed and important stage in the loan process. You have looked in the mirror, made some hard decisions, decided you do want to purchase a property, and met with a qualified, intelligent, and caring loan officer. Think about what you have read so far.

You will have accomplished a lot more than most people, and those who follow these steps almost always find that the house hunting and loan process goes smoothly. (If you have the time, re-read this chapter. Make sure you understand what you need to do.)

Finally, here is a review of the essential points:

1. Do not look for a home until you are fully pre-approved.

2. Do not get fully pre-approved until you have decided on a maximum monthly payment.

3. Always meet with a loan officer in person.

4. Only sign an application, disclosures, and GFE if you understand everything and are truly ready to buy a house.

Chapter 5:
Finding a House and Applying
for a Loan (For Real)

Why Shouldn't You Have Fun?

Now the fun begins. You have been pre-approved and are ready to close on the house. Well, almost ready. I suppose you do need to find your house first.

You and your loan officer have discussed your financing, and you should have a good idea of the price for the house that you will buy. It's time to meet with your realtor to discuss your ideal house.

A good buyer's agent should call the loan officer to discuss the pre-approval letter and ask how the loan officer evaluated the borrower's loan and any other relevant questions. It is not necessary for the agent to know all of the financial, personal details about the borrower, but a good agent will probably ask if everything is in line, if the loan officer met with the client and reviewed all of the documents, and if the loan officer now has all the documents to write a pre-approval letter. Imagine how happy your realtor will be when you hand him your legitimate pre-approval letter. It is a realtor's nightmare to represent you in making a purchase offer on a property only to find out that the pre-approval was not legitimate, but only a piece of paper with unsubstantiated words.

But you're different. You completed your homework before you started shopping for a house. You have shown the realtor that you are responsible; she knows that you are a truly qualified buyer, and she will research prospective houses longer and harder for a client like you.

Most important, when you are ready to make an offer on a property, your realtor can give the seller's agent your pre-approval letter demonstrating that your offer is solid and desirable.

You've made an offer on a house you can afford. This is the nail-biting part of the house search. You have made an offer and are waiting for the seller's response. Many times the process takes a series of offers and counteroffers. Eventually (hopefully) your offer will be accepted. The agents will write a contract, which both the buyers and sellers will sign. The seller will also require *earnest money*—good faith money that the seller's agent will hold in return for taking the property off the market while the buyer's mortgage loan is being processed and approved. At the closing, you will get this money back (under most circumstances). In some states, laws require an attorney to be present at the closing, and so the attorneys will review the contract when it is ready for signing, to make sure that everything is satisfactory and the terms are in their client's best interest. This is known as the *attorney review period*.

While the attorney review period takes place, the buyer should get an *inspection* of the property. An inspector examines the condition of the house. You are trying to find out if the structure, maintenance, and other aspects of the house are in good shape. The inspector has nothing to do with determining the value of the house.

If there are some major or minor issues with the house, your agent will discuss them with the seller's agent, who will then discuss them with the seller. Sometimes the attorneys get involved. Once any final conditions of the contract are agreed on, including any inspection issues, the contract is finalized, and the buyers and sellers will either sign a revised contract or initial and date any changes or additional terms to the original signed document.

Both sides have agreed to the terms and have finalized the purchase price, terms, and closing date. If the buyer now backs out of the contract, once the attorney review period has passed (which is usually about five days after the signing of the contract), the seller has the right to keep the buyer's earnest money.

Nevertheless, you have decided to make that bungee jump.

LOCKING THE LOAN

At this time it is critical to be sure that you are happy with your loan officer. You should make a commitment to help each other during the process. Once the loan officer starts the process, you should be clear that you have entered a two-way partnership.

By going through the pre-approval process, you have provided much of the information needed to make your loan. However, depending on how much time has elapsed and any questions that may arise, the loan officer may need additional information or documents. Bear in mind that his ability to serve you well relies on your commitment to provide any additional information needed in a complete and timely manner.

The next step is to review the mortgage program that you have chosen so that your loan officer can secure your funds, the terms, and interest rate for the loan. This is called *locking the loan*.

The loan officer is getting a commitment from the end lender to "hold" the loan for a certain number of days at the interest rate that is available on the day the loan officer is locking. Standard lock periods for finished construction are for fifteen, thirty, forty-five, and sixty days. (There are even longer locks of more than one year, which are great for new construction.)

You must close on your new property within that number of days from the lock date. If you go past the expiration date, you must either relock the loan at the then current market rate or pay for an extension. Locking your loan at the right time is critical—especially where new construction is concerned and delays seem inevitable.

Now that the loan is locked, and the loan officer has provided in writing verification of the terms of the lock, the loan officer can begin the second stage of the loan process. If several months have passed since you supplied the documentation for your pre-approval, the loan officer will request updated documents. He will then organize and re-verify all of the borrower's documents, including the credit report, the application, and the rate lock, and submit the file to his analyst (sometimes referred to as a processor).

It is the analyst's job to review the entire file thoroughly and make sure that the information is entered on the application properly, that all necessary documents have been provided, and that the file is ready to be submitted for underwriting. This is a critical step, because if something is overlooked at this point, it may not show up until shortly before closing, which can cause the closing to be postponed.

APPRAISING THE SITUATION

Before the analyst can submit the file to underwriting, an *appraisal* must be ordered. An appraisal is a market valuation of the property. A licensed, independent appraiser will visit the property to review the size, dimensions, number of bedrooms, and other characteristics of the property and then compare it to other similar properties within an approximate one-half- to one-mile radius.

The appraiser's job is to make sure that the house is worth the purchase price. For example, if you are buying a hi-rise condo that is 1,200 square feet, two bedrooms, two bathrooms, a balcony, and a deeded parking space, the appraiser is going to find at least three other properties (in this case probably one within the condo complex and two outside the complex) that are as close as possible in dimensions and characteristics to your condo.

Sometimes it may be difficult to find comparable properties (often referred to as *comps*), and this can create problems in getting a loan approved. In addition, if the subject property has very unique characteristics, the value may be difficult to compare. Most of the time, though, the property will appraise at market value without any problems in finding comps.

Every now and then the appraised value comes in lower than the purchase price, and at that point the borrower needs to decide if he wants to continue with the purchase. Underwriters will always use the *lower* of the purchase price or the appraised value when determining LTV. For example, if the purchase price is $250,000 and the appraisal is $255,000, then an underwriter is going to use the $250,000 for loan to value purposes and everything is straightforward for the borrower. If, however, the purchase price is $250,000 and the appraisal comes in at $245,00, the underwriter would use $245,000 in determining LTV, and so no matter what the down payment will be, the borrower will still need to bring an additional $5,000 to cover the difference between the appraisal and purchase price.

Here is another way of looking at this. If the purchase price is $300,000 and the appraisal comes in at $280,000, the buyer has two options. He can try to renegotiate with the seller to lower the purchase price, or he can continue the purchase of the property at the $300,000 purchase price. And here is the issue: If the borrower plans to put down 20 percent ($60,000, based on the purchase price of $300,000), the new down payment would have to be $56,000 (20 percent of $280,000) plus an additional $20,000 to cover the purchase price of $300,000, for a total of $76,000.

Once the appraisal comes back to the analyst, all the documents are ready to be sent to and reviewed by the underwriter.

THE DAY OF JUDGMENT

The underwriter verifies all the documents and guidelines for lender approval. The underwriter double checks the loan officer's choice of loan programs and compares the borrower's documents (pay stubs, tax returns, and asset statements), the stated information on the application, the credit report, and the appraisal to the loan program guidelines.

Additionally, the underwriter uses the automated underwriter report from the pre-approval process as a guide for this final underwriting review. However, there is some subjective decision making that is the underwriter's responsibility. If the borrower's asset statements show very large, unusual deposits (unusual for the level of income stated on the application), an underwriter, per basic underwriting guidelines, can question the deposits and require the borrower to explain them.

As I mentioned earlier, with most conventional loan programs the borrower must use only her own money (or a gift from a family member) for down payment and closing costs as well as for asset verification. The underwriter will want to make sure that unusual deposits are the borrower's own sources of income.

Think back. Who should have anticipated this problem? Right. The loan officer should have picked this up at the time of application and discussed it with the borrower. Maybe the borrower's mother and father gave her the money as a gift for down payment (which is fine), but this gift would need to be documented. Now the underwriter is going to require a completed gift form and probably a paper trail to verify the origination of the gift, a copy of the check (written by the parents), and a copy of the deposit slip for the borrower's savings account.

These steps take time. A good loan officer will catch this kind of thing during the pre-approval process and will ask the borrower for the appropriate documentation to avoid a mad scramble two weeks before the loan is scheduled to close.

Another example of the underwriter's discretion involves the borrower's income. Most of the time, a borrower who is paid salary must only provide thirty days' worth of pay stubs.

However, if the borrower is commissioned, and that commission amount is 100 percent of the income, there may be other considerations. If the loan officer used the same requirements for this borrower (two pay stubs), the underwriter is going to have a problem. Most loan programs require that borrowers whose commission income is greater than 25 percent of her total income provide documentation of one full year of income (the previous year's tax returns) plus the current year-to-date income. The qualifying income is calculated by dividing the total number of months of income that was used into the total income amount.

Sometimes the loan program requires two years of tax returns. If the loan officer used just the last thirty days of income to calculate the borrower's qualification ratios (remember the debt-to-income averages we talked about), and this was by far the highest commission earned over the last fourteen months, the borrower may have a much higher debt-to-income ratio than the loan officer figured originally.

Sound complicated? It can get that way. That's one more reason to carefully choose a professional, experienced loan officer.

AND THE ANSWER IS ...

Once the underwriter validates all the information, she will make an underwriting decision. An underwriter's approval allows the loan to progress to the closing stage. Basically the underwriter can make four decisions:

1. *Approval with no conditions:* the underwriter has verified and examined the entire file. Everything passes the program's and the underwriter's guidelines, and the underwriter does not need any further documents. The underwriter has cleared the loan to proceed to the closing stage, and so the loan is clear to close.

2. *Approval with conditions:* the underwriter has verified and examined the file. The loan may be approved, although certain conditions must be satisfied for closing. It is kind of like the underwriter saying, "I'll approve this loan on the condition that ...." The condition may be minor, like

providing a more recent pay stub or asset statement, or it could be more substantial, like explaining a large deposit in an asset account, something that a borrower may not be able to do. Usually, however, if the loan officer has done his job, the only conditions—if there are any—will be minor.

3. *Decline:* the underwriter may find that certain information is not accurate or does not pass the guidelines. For example, if the guidelines call for a maximum DTI of 45 percent, and the DTI on the application is 48 percent, the underwriter will decline the loan. There may be other reasons for a decline. Once again, the loan officer should have caught this at the beginning of the loan process and put the borrower into a program that would allow for a higher DTI.

4. Suspend: the underwriter may not outright decline the loan but may suspend it, asking for certain clarifications before making a decision. For example, the underwriter may see that the borrower has multiple large deposits in an asset account, and instead of approving the loan, the underwriter may hold off and ask for the borrower to write a letter of explanation. If the letter satisfies the underwriter, the loan would be approved, otherwise the underwriter may decline the loan or request further documentation.

You need to know that most loans are approved. The majority of loans do not cause a problem, though, as I stated at the beginning of the book, the end result—the underwriter's final judgment—really rests on the loan officer's shoulders. If the loan officer collects all the documents, enters the borrower's information accurately, and calculates and chooses the loan program with attention, the loan should be approved with a clear to close.

CLOSING

Now that the loan has been cleared to close, the borrower's file will go to the closing department where certain final documents will be examined and the closing documents will be drawn.

The lender will examine the insurance policy to make sure there is sufficient coverage. As I mentioned earlier, for a single-family house or multi-unit property, the borrower must purchase coverage for one year up front. This insurance will protect the borrower in the event that the property is damaged or destroyed.

If the borrower is purchasing a condominium, insurance for the exterior structure is covered by the condo or homeowners' association, and so the lender is going to require a copy of the certificate of insurance from the association. The lender will verify that the association has sufficient and correct coverage. Townhouses can be a little tricky in that some do not require insurance, and some do. The borrower should ask the loan officer at the beginning stages of the process what insurance coverage will be required.

The closing department will also reexamine the *title report* to make sure there are no existing claims to the property. The title verifies previous ownership and any claims to the property such as mortgages or other liens that someone may have placed. All claims must be cleared, and the current owner must waive the right to all claims to the property.

Once the closing department clears the insurance policy and the title report, the closing documents will be drawn up. Theoretically, the review of insurance and title at a good mortgage lender should be done at the beginning of the underwriting process, though sometimes the documents are not available, and so the closing department will make sure that these steps are not overlooked.

While the closing department is preparing to draw the closing documents, the closer—the actual person from the lender who will work with the title company on closing the loan—will review the GFE and make sure that all the costs are accounted for. The GFE and certain disclosures that the borrower signed at the time of application tell the closer what documents to print as well as what monetary figures to send to the title company. The closer will send the lender costs, escrow amount, and other amounts to be received or paid to the title company, who in turn will collect these amounts, as well as any amounts that the seller's attorney will send, to create the settlement statement (one document) for both the buyer and seller to sign. The settlement statement itemizes who receives funds and who owes funds.

The closer will print out the full closing packet with all the documents that the buyer will sign at closing. Depending on the lender, the closer may either have a check created for the loan amount payable to the title company or may have a wire sent via electronic courier. The money for the loan, one way or another, should be available at the time of the closing, which is usually the next day.

For people who are selling and buying a home on the same day, I have one comment: if possible, don't do it. Though buyers and sellers do this successfully all the time, there are probably just as many cases where people, for various reasons, fail to close on the sale of their property in the morning and, as a result, lack the money for the purchase of their new home in the afternoon. This can cause anxiety, broken contracts, and unexpected expenses.

If possible, allow a couple of days between the day you sell your current property and the day you purchase your new home. Then, if there is a delay, you will have those buffer days to get everything in order and get the funds for the purchase.

So now that you are getting ready to close the loan and get the keys to your house, aren't you glad you were pre-approved? Imagine finding out a day or two before closing that you were not pre-approved correctly, or that some information is missing, or that ANYTHING would stop you from closing on your new home. Unfortunately, it happens too often.

But for you, the person who has done all the correct things, everything is ready to close.

THE BUNGEE "BOING"

I remember clearly—after I had jumped and was falling—waiting to hear the bungee make the "boing," the sound of the cord catching, stretching, and bouncing me back up. I knew that once I heard this sound, things would be okay again, and I was not going to die a bungee death. The sound never came. But I sure felt the "catch" of the bungee, and that was enough for me.

It is right around the time of closing that most home buyers are feeling the "boing." For some, the moment comes when they hear that the loan is clear to close. For others, it is when they go to the title company and see everyone there and the documents all ready to be signed. Still, for others, it does not come until every document is signed and the closer at the title company says, "The loan is funded."

FUN FOR EVERYONE

The closing should be a fun occasion. For many people, because they are still waiting for the "boing," they feel tension and anxiety, and they do not enjoy the moment. Nevertheless, if everyone has done a great, competent job—loan officer, realtor, attorney, appraiser, inspector, title company, loan analyst, underwriter, and closing department—the closing should be smooth and without any trouble.

As I have mentioned, some states require the presence of an attorney. Some do not, and the closer at the title company will explain the documents that the buyer and seller will sign. In other states, the buyer and seller will have an attorney to serve the same function.

Really, the most important thing is to have a good pen and stamina. You will need to sign a stack of documents. Everything else will be done for you.

It is not uncommon for people to find out at the closing table that the loan is not going to close for various reasons. The lender may not have had an actual clear to close but told everyone that the loan was cleared with the hopes that things would be resolved in time. There may be an issue with the funding (usually when the wire is delayed by hours, perhaps even a day or two), or, as the borrower is signing documents, the lender costs have changed, and the borrower now learns that the lender is charging more money. The only way to avoid this scenario, as I have emphasized, is to have chosen a great loan officer.

SIGNING ON THE DOTTED LINE

Now it just comes down to signing the documents. Here are the most important:

1. *HUD-1* (Settlement Statement) has all the credits and costs for both the buyer and seller, and will show who will receive money for what and who owes money and for what. The bottom line shows how much money the buyer and seller need to either bring to closing or will be receiving at closing.

2. *Promissory Note* is the borrower's promise to repay the loan and under what terms.

3. *Mortgage* is the actual loan that uses the property as collateral.

4. *Truth-in-Lending (TIL)* is the document, which you should have first received within three days of completing the loan application, that provides information about your particular loan, such as the total cost of your loan given as the annual percentage rate (APR), the amount financed, as well as other terms.

5. *Disclosures*, some of which you have already signed at the application.

Have patience and make sure you understand the documents you are signing. Ask to have anything explained until you understand it to your satisfaction. Now is the time to have things understood because we are almost ...

AT THE END

Bravo! You have signed the documents and have given the closer your certified bank check for down payment and closing costs, and now the closer at the title company will fax the important documents to the lender. Once the lender approves that everything is in order, they authorize the title company to fund the loan (use the money that the lender has sent, via wire or other payment method, to pay out the appropriate settlement costs as represented on the HUD 1 form).

You now own your new house!

WHAT, THERE'S MORE?

Before you leave the title company, make sure you have a package of all the documents that you have signed. You will need them for future reference, especially if you ever refinance the property you just bought. Take a card from the title company and get the closer's name just in case there are any issues.

Finally, make sure you have all the keys to the new house. And the remote control if you have a garage.

EVALUATE YOUR LOAN OFFICER

After a few weeks have passed and you have moved in and have settled down from the closing and moving process, review how things went regarding your loan officer. Did everything go smoothly? Did the loan officer deliver everything that was promised? Did you feel that he was in control and knew what he was doing? Was he pleasant and personable? Did he have your best interests at heart?

Most important, would you refer this person to a friend or relative? Loan officers work through referrals. If you loved working with your loan officer, tell everyone you know to call him or her when they are considering purchasing or refinancing a home. As you now know, loan officers work hard. They like to be rewarded with personal referrals from satisfied clients.

WOULD YOU JUMP AGAIN?

Now that you have made this jump, would you do it again? Buying a home and getting a mortgage to buy the home should be smooth, but you now know that there can be bumps in the road. And now that you have made that bungee jump, isn't it worth it? And wasn't that fun?

Please let me know if this book has been helpful, and if you have any comments or suggestions please contact me at www. RichardCohenonline.com.

And again: Congratulations!

When Things Go Wrong

You have read this book and feel that you have done all the right things, found a house, and started the loan process. Yet a problem pops up.

Whether the issue seems small or overwhelming, where the mortgage process is concerned, little problems tend to bulge and grow, causing more issues. What do you do?

Following are things that I have found to be common issues. Some may be lender-related and can be addressed to your loan officer, though sometimes an attorney should get involved. In any case, do not let things go too far, and address them directly and immediately.

I contacted a loan officer and got a pre-approval. After I found a home, the loan officer started the process, but just a few days before closing, the loan officer told me that the loan was not approvable. I feel as though the pre-approval process and the pre-approval letter was a joke. How could I have prevented this?

> As I mentioned earlier in this book, meet with your loan officer. Ask him a lot of questions. Also, question the person who is referring the loan officer to you. Ask more questions. Usually the problems stem from the buyer not taking her time to meet with the loan officer in person and discuss what's involved in the pre-approval process.

Remember: your loan officer should be asking (and answering) a lot of questions and should be requesting and reviewing all of your documents. Anything less can get you in this (bad) situation.

I was very excited about the new home, but got a call from my loan officer that the property appraised at a lower amount than the purchase price. What do I do now?

You can cancel the deal, make up the difference between the purchase price and the appraised value from your own pocket, or try to negotiate with the seller to lower the price. Explain to the seller that comparable properties are not giving the higher value of the original purchase price. If a seller is motivated, you may get him to lower the purchase price.

While reviewing the HUD-1 (the final settlement statement) at the closing, I found that the lender fees were much higher than what were on the original Good Faith Estimate. What can I do?

It may be a legitimate error that the title company can correct easily. First, if the loan officer is not present, contact him to discuss the issue. If, however, the loan officer is now telling you different information than was conveyed either verbally or in writing at the application (and on the GFE), you now have two options. You can close the loan, or you can decide not to close, find another loan officer with another lender, and close later. Obviously, there are ramifications with either choice. Clearly, at this point you will have to spend more money (new lender fees, attorney fees, seller fees, etc.) that you never anticipated.

At the application I chose a fixed-rate mortgage, and when I got to the closing I found out that I was signed up for an adjustable-rate mortgage. Can I get this changed?

> Call your loan officer. If she tells you that you in fact did choose an ARM, hopefully you have the disclosure from the application that shows what program you chose and that you actually signed the disclosures to verify that program. There may have been a legitimate mistake where the lender can redraw (reprint) the documents and e-mail or fax them to the title company. If the loan officer is not cooperative, you have to choose between closing and not closing.

I finished signing all the documents and found out that I would not be able to get the keys to my new house until the next day. Turns out that the lender had problems wiring (sending) the money. How can I avoid that next time?

> Work with a lender who does not wire funds. Sometimes you will have a "dry closing," where you will sign all the documents but receive ownership the next day when the wire arrives to fund the loan. When you work with a broker, the end lender wires the money, whereas a banker, who funds the loan directly, will have a check available at the closing. (Sometimes the bank will have to wire the funds. An out-of-state loan may be an example.)

FREQUENTLY ASKED QUESTIONS

(Some More Frequent Than Others)

1. **Do I need a real estate agent?**

   You absolutely do not need *any* real estate agent. But you do need a *great* one. You want the agent's experience and expertise to help you select the neighborhood and the home. A great agent will shorten the time it takes to locate a home, and once you find a home, the agent will lead the way in the negotiation process. You don't want to negotiate directly with an experienced agent who is representing the seller. You will not understand the process and will not know how to negotiate the best deal for yourself. Your agent will do this. In addition, your agent will handle all the paperwork that can become confusing and frustrating.

2. **People tell me to *shop* around. You are telling me to be careful. What is the best way to approach this?**

   It is perfectly fine to shop around. My concern is that people shop for a mortgage as though it were a commodity. The main point of this book is to explain that though interest rates between two, three, or four lending institutions may be the same, the skill and knowledge and ability to take care of you and your loan vary drastically. You have to shop wisely and carefully.

3. What are valid lender costs?

This is hard to say. In general, the lender will have costs anywhere from $500 to $1,500 (application fee, processing fee, rate lock deposit, etc.). The question you should ask yourself is if you feel it will be worth paying more money because you want the expertise and service that the loan officer offers. As I mentioned at the beginning of the book, would you spend a few hundred dollars more for a doctor or attorney? You want to make sure that the loan officer has explained all the costs and commits them in writing on the GFE. If something does not sound right, question the numbers. And never accept verbal answers. You have no protection.

4. Is it okay to have my credit run several times by different lenders?

It depends. If you already have good credit, having your credit run a few times will not hurt your score. If, however, you already have poor credit, there is a great possibility that the multiple credit reports could lower your score, especially if you have had your credit run many times in a 12-month period prior to the mortgage inquiries. Lenders get nervous when borrowers have applied for many credit accounts (credit cards, automobiles, mortgages), and so if you are thinking of buying a home, be careful how often you inquire about other new debt and having your credit run to acquire new credit accounts.

5. If I have poor credit, can I get this fixed?

A good loan officer can offer advice about how to improve your credit score. A great loan officer may even offer to help, although in any case the borrower has to do most of the work. Once the credit problems are cleared, there is no way to predict how long it will take before the credit scores improve. In general, the worse the credit and the more problems on the report, the longer it will take for the scores to improve.

6. I have heard that some loan officers charge points. What does this mean?

A point is a percentage of the loan amount. One point on a $200,000 loan equals $2,000. You will see full points and percentages of points (for example 1/8 of a point, 1/4 of a point, etc.).

A loan officer can charge an origination point, which is a way to charge for the cost of writing the loan. Borrowers can also pay a discount point, which is a fee paid to lower the interest rate of the loan. The way end-lenders pay loan officers to close and to process loans is through a commission structure. The more risky the loan, the lower the commission amount, and so the loan officer may need to charge an origination fee to earn compensation for making and processing the loan.

If a borrower wants to "buy down" the interest rate, they can often do that by paying a discount point. For example, if the quoted interest rate for the loan you chose is 7.00 percent, you can pay a discount point (or portion of a discount point) up front to lower the rate, for example, to 6.625 percent. To know if this is a good investment or not, the borrower should figure out the difference between total interest that you would pay over the life of the loan at the higher interest rate compared to the interest at the lower interest rate plus the amount of the discount point. There is a break-even time, where paying a point or portion of a point for a discounted rate makes sense. The main thing is that you understand whether your loan officer is charging discount or loan origination points. Ask the question right up front and make sure you receive an explanation that satisfies you. These amounts should always appear on the GFE.

7. Why are rates higher for longer lock periods?

The lender earns its profit through the interest charged to the borrower. The lender has a pretty good idea of the rates for tomorrow, has less of an idea about next week, and even less of an idea about thirty days from now. So the lender is going to offer slightly higher rates for longer locks to protect their return from a worsening market (interest rates going higher).

8. Is insurance required for my personal property that is inside the house?

The lender is not going to require that you purchase insurance for your personal property. The lender will only require that you purchase homeowners' insurance to insure the building that is collateral for the loan. I would highly recommend, however, that you have insurance for your personal property.

9. When should I choose private mortgage insurance (PMI)?

Look at financial examples to see what works for you. There are ways other than PMI to structure loans if the borrower has less than 20 percent down payment. You can do a combination first and second mortgage, the first at 80 percent LTV, and then a second mortgage for the remainder of the total loan amount. You can also do lender-paid mortgage insurance, where the borrower does not pay the mortgage insurance, and the lender will raise the rates slightly to compensate.

Also, you can do financed mortgage insurance, where the amount of mortgage insurance that you would pay before you would reach 78 percent LTV, is incorporated into the loan. No one option is right for everyone. Each borrower must look at the financial cases to see what works best for them. Each option has pros and cons. No one option is right for everyone. This is an area in which a great loan officer can help you understand the alternatives and the implications of each.

10. Can I negotiate the lender costs?

You can certainly try. Some loan officers will do anything—and often promise anything—to get your business. Nobody offers loans for free. Think about it.

11. Do I have to bungee jump before I buy a home?

Absolutely not! I'll be happy to send you a copy of my bungee jump video. Live vicariously.

If Interest Rate is not the Most Important Thing, What is?

1. That depends. Really, in the end, *your priorities* are the most important reason to select a program and/or interest rate. You need to ask yourself what is the most important thing for *you*. Having the lowest monthly payment? Having money left over after the closing to decorate your home? Paying off the mortgage in the shortest amount of time?

2. As I have mentioned directly throughout the book, interest rate is important, but the more important question is who will be working with you regarding the loan. You need help, and you need guidance. The lowest interest rate in the world cannot help a loan that does not get approved or does not close on time due to loan officer error or incompetence. Remember that you have the control to decide with whom you will work. Take your time and make sure that that person is the right person for you.

3. Is it possible to have both a great rate and a great loan officer? Absolutely. If this is what you want, then

you should make sure that *nothing* deters you from accomplishing this goal.

Appendix A

Things You'll Need for Your Pre-approval Consultation

Group 1: Essential Documents

1. Last two years' federal tax returns with W-2s
2. Thirty days of pay stubs
3. Sixty days of consecutive asset statements with all numbered pages including blank pages
4. Driver's license or state ID card

Group 2: Less Essential Documents; Probably Required

1. Landlord's name and telephone phone number (if renting)
2. Current mortgage payment, tax, and insurance information (if currently own a property)

3. Employer's information for the previous two years

4. Residence information for the previous two years

5. Divorce degree if alimony or child support is involved

GROUP 3: FOR CERTAIN SITUATIONS

1. Addresses, values, programs, rates, taxes, and insurance premiums (all relevant information) for any investment/ rental properties currently owned

2. Verification of satisfied liens, collections, judgments, or bankruptcies that may appear on the credit report

3. If getting a gift for down payment and/or closing costs, the name, address, and phone number of the person giving the gift

Appendix B
Steps in the Loan Process

1. Decide on a budget that will include your total monthly mortgage (including assessment if applicable)

2. Decide if buying a home is right for you

3. Collect documents required for pre-approval consultation

4. Meet with a loan officer to get pre-approved

5. Decide if buying a home is still right for you

6. Review and sign loan application documents

7. Meet with real estate agent

8. Meet with an attorney, if applicable

9. Find your home, write a contract, negotiate, and agree on terms

10. Schedule and complete home inspection

11. Meet with loan officer to review loan program terms and lock loan

12. Send contracts to attorney for review, if applicable

13. Lender orders appraisal

14. Loan goes to underwriting on receipt of appraisal

15. Loan approval (perhaps with conditions)

16. Satisfy conditions, if applicable

17. Obtain homeowners' insurance, if applicable

18. Go to bank for closing funds, if applicable

19. Closing at the title company

20. Fly to Queenstown to see what is more thrilling: buying a home or bungee jumping

Index

title xiii, 13, 18, 41, 42, 55, 56, 57,
    59, 62, 63, 76
title company 13, 42, 55, 56, 57, 59,
    62, 63, 76
title insurance 41
title report 55
Trans Union 24
Truth-in-Lending (TIL) 58
type of property 32

U
underwrite 27
underwriter 7, 8, 9, 11, 27, 28, 29,
    41, 51, 52, 53, 54, 57
underwriting 2, 8, 9, 16, 40, 41, 50,
    52, 53, 55, 75
underwriting software 9
unit 32, 55
units 31, 32

V
verification 1, 8, 27, 41, 50, 52
verify 1, 7, 9, 11, 15, 24, 26, 29, 30,
    42, 50, 52, 55, 63

W
W-2 11, 73
W-2s 27, 73
wire 56, 58, 59, 63
wiring 63

ABOUT THE AUTHOR

Richard Cohen's new book, "It's Not About Rate: The Right Way to Get a Mortgage," is the culmination of thousands of conversations with new homebuyers. The book is intended to convey a comprehensive yet basic understanding of the mortgage process and the best way to approach it.

Richard lives with his wife and daughter in Chicago, IL. He looks forward to his next bungee jump.

For more information, visit his website at www.RichardCohenOnline.com

www.ingramcontent.com/pod-product-compliance
Lightning Source LLC
Chambersburg PA
CBHW022112170526
45157CB00004B/1592